D1436557

LAMBORGHINI
COUNTACH

LAMBORGHINI COUNTACH

Chris Bennett

OSPREY
AUTOMOTIVE

Dedicated to all Countach owner users.

First published in
Great Britain in 1993 by Osprey
an imprint of Reed Consumer Books Limited
Michelin House, 81 Fulham Road,
London SW3 6RB
and Auckland, Melbourne, Singapore
and Toronto

© 1993 Reed International Books Limited

All rights reserved. Apart from any fair
dealing for the purpose of private study,
research, criticism or review, as permitted
under the Copyright, Design and Patents Act,
1988, no part of this publication may be
reproduced, stored in a retrieval system, or
transmitted in any form or by any means,
electronic, electrical, chemical, mechanical,
optical, photocopying, recording or otherwise,
without prior written permission. All
enquiries should be addressed to the
publisher.

ISBN 1 85532 303 6

Edited by Donna Skender
Page design by Paul Kime
Printed in China

Acknowledgements

The author would like to offer his grateful thanks to the many people who readily offered their time and vehicles, thereby making this project a reality and especially – Vic 'Red Rocket' Sawyer, Peter Hay, Steve Forster, Rick Lee, Mike Pullen of Carrera Sports in Horsham, Mike Lake, Steve Ashton, Piet Pulford and Peter Leonard-Morgan of Portman Lamborghini. Many thanks also goes to Ubaldo Sgarzi and Valentino Balboni of Automobili Lamborghini together with my good friends John Pitchforth of Nikon UK Ltd and Paul Waller of Commercial Cameras in Woking Surrey.

Half title page
Hauling down nearly a ton-and-a-half from well over twice the legal limit calls for very special braking properties. Four-pot ATE brake callipers do the business on the massive ventilated discs

Title page
Remember geometry lessons at school? Gandini obviously did, majoring on the trapezium as the styling cue to achieve the Countach shape. Its purity was somewhat compromised along the way, but the NACA cooling ducts in the flanks and the new air boxes simply served to render the car more outrageous

For a catalogue of all books published by Osprey Automotive
please write to:

**The Marketing Department, Reed Consumer Books,
1st Floor, Michelin House, 81 Fulham Road, London SW3 6RB**

About The Author

Countach is the fourth book that Chris Bennett has produced for Osprey. His first two works featured military aviation subjects involving F-15 Eagle and F-18 Hornet jet-fighters based in Germany. His third book was a pictorial tribute to the ubiquitous Land Rover. Currently he is working on a number of future aviation and automotive books, including productions involving the Range Rover, Lamborghini Diablo and Formula 1 racing teams.

All images reproduced in this volume were shot exclusively with Nikon F4s cameras, fitted with Nikkor lenses and loaded with Fuji Velvia and Kodak Kodachrome stocks.

Introduction

In today's world of extremes, the outrageous Lamborghini Countach has become a legend and an enigma. When unleashed on an unsuspecting public in 1971 the Countach was the first true road-going 'supercar' – a marvel of extremes in design and performance, as well as purchase price.

Born to the inspirational pen of Marcello Gandini the Countach has proved over the years to be a lifesaver for the Sant'Agata based Automobili Lamborghini and a persistent thorn in the side of the other, larger Italian performance car manufacturer just down the road at Modena.

Currently, in addition to Lamborghini and Ferrari, there is an increasing number of other manufacturers and young contenders, all vying for the super-car crown. Each of these are intent on pitching for a slice of the lucrative market that caters to the well-healed and extravagant, with price tags to match.

With many years of continuous development culminating in the 25th Anniversary model, Lamborghini have sadly ceased production of the venerable Countach, the last examples exiting the factory in July 1990. In its place stands a new, faster and still reassuringly expensive projectile called the Diablo.

For many, however, the Countach with its extreme and aggressive angles, will always reign supreme. And, indeed, few machines can match its almost absurd ability to demand attention. This position is enhanced by the relatively few examples that can be observed, hence an almost mystic quality of admiration and envy has built up around the car and its owner.

The highly enviable state of being a Countach owner suggests a number of prerequisites. A certain amount of wealth being the obvious, as well as the ability to capitalise on the car's virtues by enjoying a degree of exhibitionism, as the Countach is guaranteed to be the centre of attention. With nearly 500bhp under the right foot it's also one of the quickest methods of banishment from the Queen's highways known to man (just ask Vic Sawyer).

Overall, as a statement of style and intent the Countach is the unchallenged leader of the pack. Few mortals can resist its throaty roar, aggressive disposition and sheer 'pulling' power. Fewer still are actually fortunate enough to own a Countach, but they persistently cultivate the dream that maybe one day...

This book is for the smitten, the enthusiast and the dreamer. It's not a history of the Countach, but rather an informal and colourful portrait of both car and owner in action.

For those wishing to rub shoulders with Lamborghini personalities on a regular basis, membership of the Lamborghini Club UK is open to all (they accepted the author!). Just write to:

Mike McMahon
Lamborghini Club UK, 37 Herschell Road
Leigh-on-Sea, Essex SS9 2NH, United Kingdom

Contents

Not many bolts in the machine in the foreground; and the Skybolt aerobatic biplane is considerably slower in level flight

The Man and His 'Works'

As the years roll by, Lamborghini seems less and less the new boy. But when he came on the scene in the mid-'60s, even post-war beginners like Ferrari and Porsche were comfortably established, and makes like Maserati and Alfa Romeo were positively old stagers. If Lamborghini didn't quite upset the applecart, he did redefine the reference points for exotic grand touring cars, as well as producing what was arguably the world's first roadgoing supercar. What constitutes a supercar? The answer is, bags of muscle from an exotic multi-cylinder engine, eye-catching broad-shouldered looks, two snug seats, an uncompromising ride and scant regard for creature comforts.

It was Ferrucio Lamborghini's agricultural origins which got him started on the road to building supercars. Born in 1916 on a farm near Ferrara, north of Bologna, the young Lamborghini came naturally into contact with the growing mechanical paraphernalia of farming. After attending an industrial training college and graduating in industrial technology, he joined the Italian air force, which took him through World War Two. There he found a constant need to improvise ways of keeping aircraft operational, which provided more lessons for the future.

Lamborghini was held prisoner on Rhodes by the British for a short time, but returned to Ferrara in 1946. He found work converting redundant military vehicles into machines suitable for agriculture. This proved lucrative and the business took off. About the same time, the first Lamborghini car was born; it was based, almost inevitably, on a Fiat Topolino, with its engine size increased from 500cc to 750cc. In 1948, with Baglioni as co-driver, Lamborghini took on the awesome Mille Miglia race. The car was retired, but a number of interested parties asked for copies. Tractors took precedence however, and in 1949 he set up his own factory appropriately called Lamborghini Trattici. There would be no more cobbled-up military conversions as the new plant would produce new tractors from the ground up. Within a decade, production was around 10 units a day.

In 1959, Lamborghini Bruciatori was formed. The company diversified into the home heating and industrial air-conditioning industry. Lamborghini was successful in this venture as he took good care of the after-sales service. It was boom time in Italy and as his business expanded Lamborghini had been able to sample several of the high performance cars of the day. As things were looking good in both enterprises, he was able to turn his attention to building his own

Countach bodies are hand-made at the spacious Sant'Agata factory, situated in sun-baked farmland between Modena and Bologna. A bodyshell has just been united with chassis, and adjustments are made to the rear

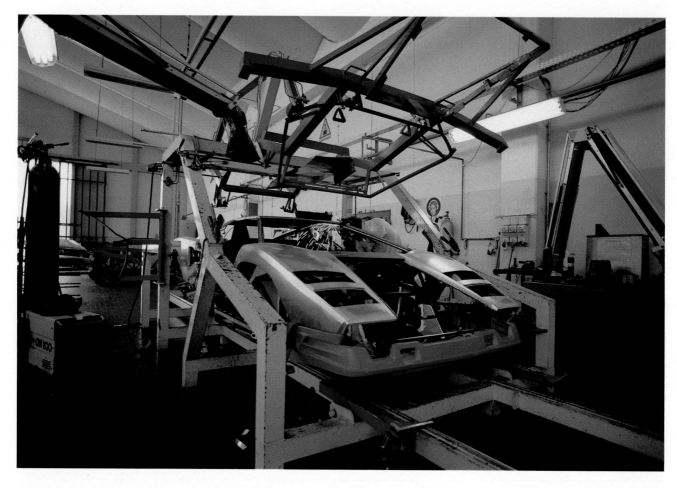

Above
Countach gets off to a good start on the 'U' shape production line. Placement within the jig ensures correct and accurate alignment of front sub-frame and upper body frame with chassis prior to welding. The upper frame acts as a built in roll-cage. These photographs feature some of the very last Countachs built, examples of the 25th Anniversary model designed to celebrate Lamborghini's quarter century as a motor manufacturer

Right
Fabricators carefully check the fit of the aluminium panels at the rear. The one-piece plastic front panel incorporates brake cooling ducts. Normally three or four men work at each of the assembly stages. After the last 25th Anniversary Countach left the production line, on 4th July 1990, they turned their hands to its successor the Diablo, or Devil

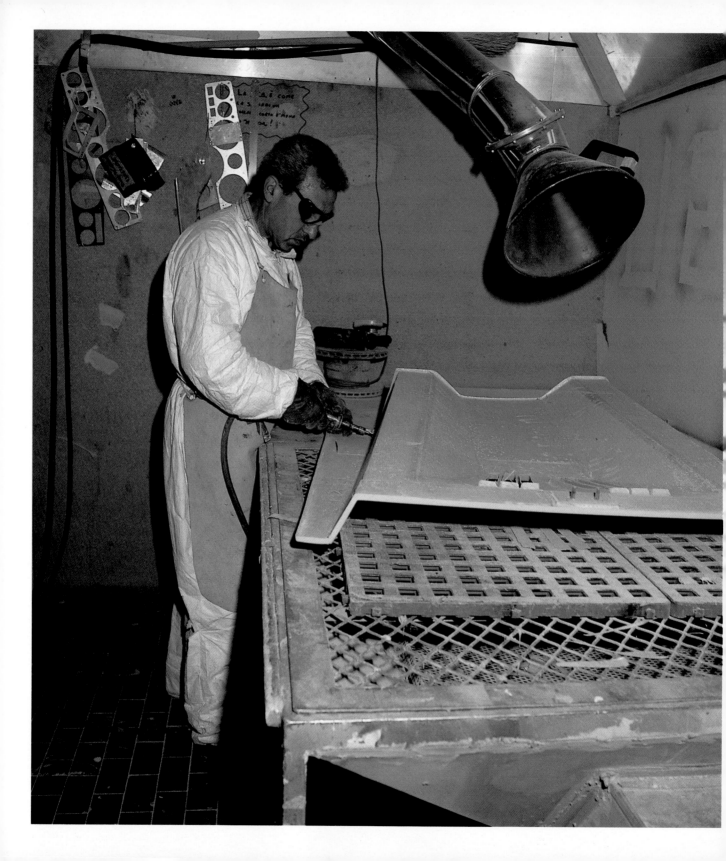

Forming the engine cover in one of the glass-fibre departments. Protection for the operator and suitable ventilation are crucial in a working environment. Note the dashboard facias hanging on the back wall. This is one of the few Countach panels to include the slats which covered Gandini's inspirational Carabo

Grand Touring car. He was keen to produce something without the faults he had come across in certain models, not least in after-sales support, and accordingly was particularly keen to show Maranello what was what. Like sports-racing car builder and tuner Carlo Abarth whose badge was the Scorpion, Lamborghini chose his own astrological sign for his company logo: Taurus the Bull. And in a typically bullish way, he tackled the prancing horse head on.

In 1963, he founded Automobili Ferrucio Lamborghini SpA, and a brand new factory was built at Sant'Agata Bolognese, only a stones throw from the shrines of Modena and Maranello. The homes of Maserati and Ferrari, hallowed names at the time. Astonishingly, when most firms take years to produce a winning formula, he got his sums right first time and came up with the 350GTV, which was shown at the Turin show in 1963. The body was built by Franco Scaglione, and it was powered by a 3.5-litre 360bhp V12, the brainchild of Ing. Giotto Bizzarrini; the latter was no mean GT car builder, a one-time Alfa and Ferrari employee and designer of the Iso Rivolta. The sophisticated four-cam motor had been devised as a Formula 1 engine, but there were no takers, so Bizzarrini took it to Lamborghini and it was scaled-up for production and use in the new 350GTV. In charge of chassis development was Gianpaolo Dallara, aged 25, an engineering graduate also with Maserati, Ferrari and Iso connections, and he produced a dynamically versatile package. Both coach builders Zagato and Touring of Milan were commissioned to produce bodies. The contract went to Touring for the production version with its distinctive oval headlights, launched in 1964.

Aware of the shortcomings of other manufacturers, Lamborghini was a stickler for quality control, and addressed his workforce as though he was a customer. He had set the stage for a line of performance cars which offered quality engineering, fine handling, high fashion and stunning looks. In the first year, 150 units were built, increasing to 250 the next. Few changes were made to the 350GTV, except that the ZF gearbox was replaced by a Lamborghini-built all-synchromesh 5-speed 'box.

In 1966 came the 400GT, a handsome two-plus-two coupe, not dissimilar to the 350GTV, but with twin headlights and a 4.0-litre engine. The engine was more flexible, but handling was slightly less poised than the earlier model. This was one of Superleggera Touring's last offerings, as the firm was in trouble. For his next opus, Lamborghini went to Bertone. The resulting creation was to revolutionise sports car design. As the first of the modern generation of supercars, it was Lamborghini's personal fighting bull, the Miura.

What was special about the P400 Miura was that it brought mid-engined sports-racing car layout to the street. The Ford GT40 did this too, in a limited way, but it was essentially a racer, lacking the up-market cachet of Lamborghini. The 4.0-litre V12 was arranged in the transverse position behind the passenger compartment, and the top speed was 160mph, or in Continental terms, just short of 300kmh. To this day there is mild controversy over who

Above

Among the Countach's most distinctive features are its 'butterfly-wing' doors, a pair of which are seen here waiting to be fitted. Each door frame is hand-fabricated and carefully built to precisely fit a specific body chassis. The doors pivot upwards and forwards, parallel to the car, counter-balanced by a hydro-pneumatic system

Left

As the vehicle's build programme progresses, the running gear is fitted; now it has the beautifully machined ventilated discs with their four-pot callipers, and the wiring loom is also in place. The twin headlight housings are popped up, but still void, as are the side-light and indicator spaces in front of them

styled the low, squat, yet sleek body, and possibly no other single design has been more disputed. Two young fast-rising stylists whose stars had yet to shine in public were working for Nuccio Bertone around that period; Giorgietto Giugiaro and Marcello Gandini. Inevitably, the presence of master and pupil leads to confusion over who designed what, rather like a Renaissance painting where the master had his assistants do certain pieces, but saved the best bits for himself. Giugiaro left to work for Ghia in 1965, leaving behind some designs for a mid-engined Alfa. His place was taken by Gandini, then aged 27, who had to finish the Miura design in double-quick time for the 1966 Geneva show. All three men had some claim to the design, for Nuccio Bertone argued that due

Above

Gem of the V12 brigade, a massive Countach engine is about to be installed. Lamborghini's 48-valve head 5.2-litre engine develops 455bhp, with bags of grunt low down and ample muscle at high revs. The driver and passenger certainly know it's there as it sits beyond a partition just inches behind their heads

Left

Each bank of the V12 has twin overhead camshafts, the cam covers, painted in a smart crackle-finish matt black, contrasting with the red of the plug leads. The linkage of the downdraught Weber carburettors can be seen on the right

Countach bodyshells progress down the line, at this stage all strange holes and apertures awaiting doors, lights and running gear. Red is invariably the colour chosen, with white second in the popularity spectrum, and yellow ranking a distant third

to Gandini's relative inexperience, he gave the project his final touch.

However it was Dallara who designed the chassis, and it was honed to perfection by Lamborghini's talented development driver and engineer, 25-year-old New Zealander Bob Wallace. He set up the suspension according to the requirements and abilities of each individual customer. Apart from the Fiat 850-derived headlights, its only fault was that it proved unstable at high speed when caught in a cross-wind, but when alloy wheels shod with better tyres were fitted to the Miura S, roadholding and adhesion improved.

The Marzal prototype of 1967 followed the Miura practice of transverse mid-engine layout, but with just a 2.0-litre straight-six instead of the V12. For its time it was a stylistic extravaganza, with huge gull-wing doors glazed to sill level, and this in the heady days of the mini-skirt! Its moment of glory came at the 1970 Monaco Grand Prix when Prince Rainier was driven around the circuit in it. The Marzal's production counterpart was the four-seater Espada of 1968, which shared the same body shape without the gullwing doors, but with its V12 engine front-mounted. The Islero, launched in 1969, was also retrospective in having the 4-litre engine up front, and was really the successor to the 400GT. Another two-plus-two, the Jarama, followed in 1970. By that time cars like the Islero were far too conventional for typical Lamborghini customers, who had become accustomed to dramatic styling.

Above
A technician fits the large single pantograph-type windscreen wiper. This head-on shot emphasises the shape of the front compartment, which houses the battery and hydraulic fluid reservoir. There is good access to the brake servo and steering rack as well as the heater and ventilation systems

Left
A Countach with its 'butterfly-wing' vertical hinging doors raised demonstrates that a garage with a high ceiling is necessary to avoid damage against the roof. Hydraulic struts support the doors in the open position, and are designed to counter-balance it perfectly

The looks and the performance and the handling may have been right but, now beset with industrial disputes and strikes, Lamborghinis were getting a reputation for inadequate finishing, particularly in their interiors. It was not uncommon for British buyers to take their cars straight to one of the leading coach builders such as Hoopers and have the interior torn out and replaced with something more carefully made. Meanwhile, all was not well with the Italian agricultural business as the tractor market was in decline. Lamborghini took this as his cue to retire, going back to the land to farm a vineyard from which he produced wine marketed as Bull's Blood.

He sold control of the car plant to Georges-Henri Rosetti, who came from a family of Swiss clockmakers. This was a short-lived arrangement, for Swiss-

Above
Final attention to detail as the technicians fine-tune the wiper setting and engine cover hinges. The front compartment cover, in common with the rear bootlid, is fabricated from Kevlar

Above right
An impressive sight as massed ranks of Countachs await delivery to the new owners. The floor tiles receding in perspective emphasise the geometric principles employed by Macello Gandini when designing the prototype; he based his calculations for the body on the trapezium, and the main shape sub-divides into yet more trapezes

Right
Mounted on the wall in the dispatch bay is a notice reminding test drivers of their responsibility to ensure that the customer is always satisfied (this sign translates to read 'The next test driver is the customer; make sure he is satisfied'). When the car is finished, it will be driven over a selection of local roads to check for any last-minute adjustments. When the prototype LP 500 was under development, it was taken over part of the venerable Mille Miglia route

IL PROSSIMO COLLAUDATORE É IL CLIENTE
FATE IN MODO CHE RESTI SODDISFATTO

made clocks were being challenged by Japanese products, and Rosetti's property developer associate Rene Leimer lent some financial muscle. He approached Luigi Capellini of DeTomaso to assist with marketing in the States, and a special version of the Urraco, the Silhouette, was proffered in vain. Hope for the company rested for a while on a deal in which the Giugiaro-designed BMW M1 sports-GT cars would be built by Lamborghini, but this one fell through partly because of Lamborghini's financial difficulties, and also because BMW elected to have the 400 examples built by Baur at Stuttgart. There was an abortive attempt in 1975 to persuade Grand Prix team owners Walter Wolf and David Thieme to take over, and in 1978, Lamborghini was sold to the German pair, Dr Neumann and BMW racing driver Hubert Hahne. Hahne had been Lamborghini concessionaire in Germany, and uncharacteristically came up with a facile scheme to turbocharge the Countach.

The 1970s was a difficult time for the motor industry in general, with many firms closing down, and for Lamborghini this sordid period reached its nadir when the next owner, the Hungarian-American Zoltan Reti got the company declared bankrupt. Enter the Mimram family. Twenty-five-year-old Patrick Mimram leased the Sant'Agata plant to keep the business going, and in 1980 the receivers put Lamborghini up for auction, and the Mimram family were the successful bidders.

But going back a decade, Lamborghini continued to evolve new models. In 1971 came the Urraco prototype, smaller than the Miura, and powered by a brand-new 2.5-litre V8 with gearbox mounted on the rear of the crankcase. It was capable of 140mph, handled well, and was every bit the junior supercar Lamborghini intended, although it never attained the commercial success of the Porsche 911 or classic status of the Ferrari Dino. By 1973 the oil-crisis and US Federal safety regulations were beginning to hurt, and a smaller model made sense. Dallara had moved on, temporarily as it turned out, to DeTomaso to design the Formula 1 car. His replacement Paolo Stanzani shuffled aside the Espada and Jarama and reorganised the Sant'Agata plant to get the Urraco up and running. Lamborghini's reputation still rested on the supercar. In recession there is always a select market for such a car so it was time to concentrate on the showcase model which had been under development as the Miura's successor for some time. The Countach.

Brooding outside the factory stands Walter Wolf's midnight blue Countach, with a white, late-model car behind. In 1974, Wolf was owner of the first LP 400, which was finished in a similar scheme to his Grand Prix cars. His patronage and consequent visability on the Formula 1 circuit benefitted Lamborghini considerably

Above

Exquisite white leather upholstery covers the electrically-operated seats which were introduced at the tail end of Countach production. A Pioneer speaker is discreetly housed in the lee of the door-shut panel

Left

Dramatic rear view of the Walter Wolf car, displaying the industrialist's company logo. During the turbulent mid-'70s, Walter Wolf was a potential owner of, but a deal was never struck. The Austria-Canadian tycoon owned four other Countachs during the '70s and '80s, nearly all of which were personalised versions specially developed by Chief Engineer Gianpaolo Dallara during his second stint at Sant'Agata Bolognese

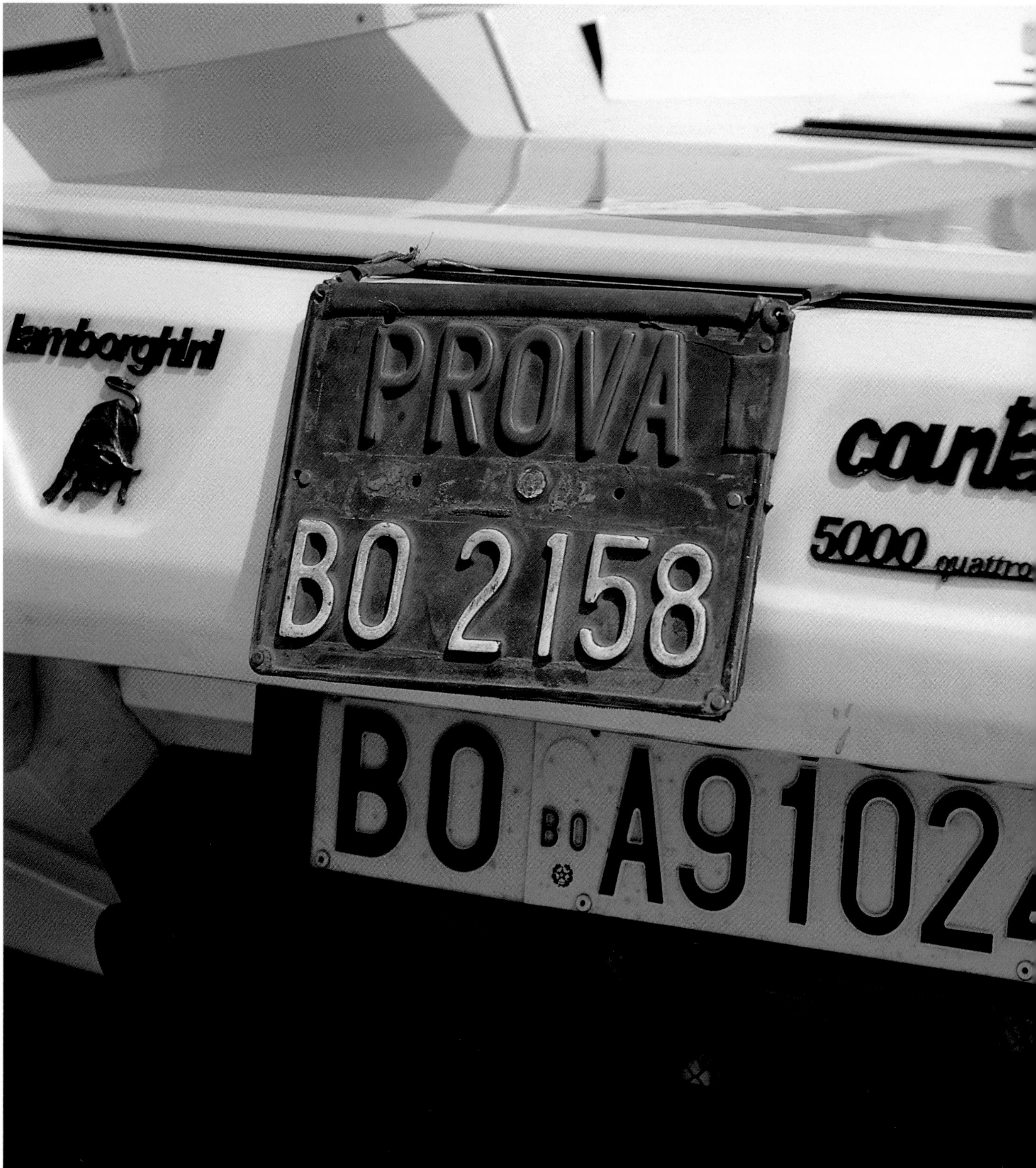
lamborghini
PROVA
BO 2158
5000 quattro

Above
A Lamborghini test driver prepares to take a 5000 Qv out for a run following a visit to the factory for maintenance. Even though the Countach is a familiar sight on the local roads, they rarely fail to turn an Italian head or two

Left
A close-up of the rear panel of a Countach, with the Lamborghini logo and signature, exclaiming it to be a US-spec 5000 quattrovalvole. The registration plates, local Bologna ones, have been supplemented with 'Prova' trade plates, installed when the car is road tested after servicing

Above
The muscular rear haunches of a car ready to pounce. The supercar equivalent of the motorcyclist's Cafe Racer, a beautiful white 25th Anniversary car poses by the shades of an Italian provincial restaurant. Many of the celebration Countachs were finished devoid of the large rear aerofoil

Left
The locals are suitably impressed as Balboni takes a well-earned break from a busy test schedule. The slatted radiator cooling duct is prominent

Above

Here sits a brave, but fortunate, man.
He may look impassive, but he regularly
hits 185mph on the Autostrada.
Valentino Balboni is Lamborghini's chief
development engineer and test driver,
and he is no stranger to topping
160mph on some of the local roads –
but it's all in a day's work. Apparently it
is not quite possible to hit the
Countach's top whack on public roads

Right

A brand new 25th Anniversary model
waits outside the factory. The rich
custard-yellow is the same colour as the
very first LP 500 prototype, driven over
the Alpine passes by tester Bob Wallace
en route the Geneva show in 1971

The Countach: Gestation Period

By 1971, when Stanzani brought out the final evolution of the Miura, the SV, the model had understandably ceased to cut the dash it did when introduced in 1966. Not only was the shape well-known, but the Miura's habit of tucking in when the throttle was lifted at high cornering speeds, plus its light front end, made a replacement inevitable. It was designated the LP 500, which stood, more or less, for Longitudinal Posteriore 5.0-litre. So Stanzani and his team opted for a different chassis and engine layout. Indeed, several important changes took place during the Countach's development. In a nutshell, the 5.0-litre engine originally used was down-sized to the previous 4.0-litre V12 as there were doubts about its reliability. The chassis was initially stressed skinned and torsion box constructed, supplanted with a multi-tubular space-frame layout. One reason for placing the engine longitudinally rather than transversely was to counteract the high-speed cross-wind behavioural inefficiency of the Miura. It also allowed for better access to all the ancillaries. The gearbox was placed ahead of the engine with a return shaft directed back through a sealed lubrication channel in the deeper, more heavily ribbed sump to the differential. The gearbox was now right by the driver's gear-changing hand, so the need for linkage control rods was removed. The powertrain was absolutely massive compared with the space occupied by the driver and passenger, with the whole emphasis of the Countach look being to bring the driving position further forward.

In a move designed to combat the stifling effect of emission controls, Stanzani went for a longer stroke 5.0-litre capacity. Initial tests were promising. Some 440bhp was recorded on the new Sant'Agata dynamometer.

Unlike the Miura, there is no question about whose hand drew the Countach. Marcello Gandini's career began in 1959 when he produced a body for an OSCA Barchetta, which taught him a great deal about vehicle construction. His big break came when Giugiaro left Bertone and he was elevated to the post of Chief Designer. At this point there were just four months to the Geneva show when the Miura was to be launched. The deadline was met and Gandini's reputation was made. Subsequent designs to come out

Lamborghini Club UK members' cars line up at the once illustrious Goodwood race track. Some people argue that there is something to be said for not attending events where such cars are present in large numbers, as the impact of an individual example is to some extent devalued. A sea of Countachs, mostly red, ensures that it is the rare or individual models which grab most of the attention. The argument wouldn't convince everybody

Above

Seen in profile, the front section of the car is one long flat plane running into the windscreen. Prominent are the side-indicator repeater, door-mounted rear-view mirror and the aftermarket split-rim wheel. The dark metallic green coachwork is refreshingly unusual

Right

A dark green Countach attempts to muscle in between two white sisters in the crowded paddock at the Goodwood meeting

of Bertone in which he had a hand included the Marzal and Espada, the Ferrari 308GT4, Maserati Khamsin, Lancia Stratos, Innocenti Mini, Fiat X-1/9, and his last commission before leaving Bertone was Citroen's widely popular BX. The family trademark is plainly visible; the front wheel arches of this family saloon are straight from the Countach. This, Gandini's most radical design, looked as outrageous in 1989 as it did in 1971. Since leaving Bertone in 1978, Gandini has worked from his villa in the wooded hills above Turin, and for five years he designed for Renault. But in 1988, he styled the dramatic V-16 Cizeta Moroder supercar (named after the Hollywood conductor) for a consortium of ex-Lamborghini employees based at Modena. Some of these people had worked on the Miura project, and certainly on the original Countach. The Cizeta could not match the Countach for looks however, appearing more like an overgrown

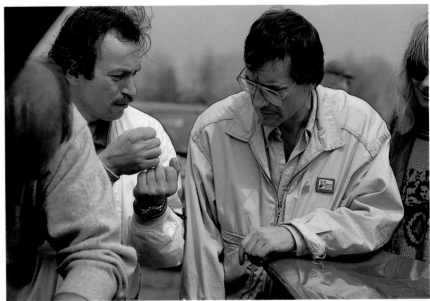

Above

Two prime movers of the Lamborghini Club UK, Mike Pullen, left, and Vic Sawyer, discuss a minor technical problem, the result of one of Vic's normal and uncompromising blasts around the Goodwood circuit. Mike was founder of the original Lamborghini Owners' Club UK, which later became known simply as the Lamborghini Club UK. He also runs Carrera Sport in Haywards Heath, and is a fund of knowledge on all matters Lamborghini

Left

It's not quite Brooklands where the 'right crowd and no crowding' motto was the order of the day, but easy-going and informal club meetings such as this one at Castle Combe give everyone a chance to check out their favourite Lamborghinis

Lotus Esprit. This was the role for Gandini's next opus for Lamborghini, the Diablo.

Back in 1971, the prototype Countach was cobbled together at the last minute, as is the way with ideas whose parameters are constantly changing, and Bob Wallace drove the custard-yellow LP500 over the snowy Alpine passes to present it at the Geneva Show. The name Countach was coined after a Torinese fabricator was heard to utter "Countach!", which roughly translated from the local patois means "Eureka!" or "That's it!"s To get the Piemontese pronunciation phonetically correct, one should say "Coontash!".

It left the world's motoring buffs reeling, so far out was the concept, both inside and out. The interior and controls were suggestive of a futuristic vehicle,

Above

The OZ telephone-dial wheels replaced similar Campagnolo rims in 1986. The difference between the later and earlier Campag styles was that on the later ones like the OZ version seen here, the ventilation and stud holes were flush with the face of the wheel, whereas the holes protruded on the earlier models. Whilst the OZ wheels are cleaner and more modern looking, the early Campags probably better suited the extrovert nature of the Countach styling. The original rear wheel arch was unadorned by the glass fibre spat which was originally introduced with the Countach LP 400 S, and its wider Pirelli P7 tyres

Rights

Like bees to a honey pot, nothing quite equals an open Countach door in attracting the fans, all keen to get a fix of that exotic V12 power-plant. This is club member Vic Sawyer's 5000 Qv at Castle Combe circuit. The letters Qv stand for quattrovalvole, meaning two inlet and two exhaust valves per combustion chamber, and as it's a V12, you get a 48-valve head

Above

A fan gets in close for a detail shot of the back panel of a winged wonder. The aerofoils which came in as options with the LP 400 S in 1977 had an angle of rake adjustment facility on the support pillar, best accessed with the luggage boot lid open

Left

These events may be thirsty work for the Lamborghini pilot, but for the Countach's V12, 'the real thing' is a 31-gallon tankful of unleaded, consumed at a rate of 17 miles per gallon. This gives a useful range of over 500 miles between stops

almost like a space ship, and based on the ideas of journalist Gianni Rogliatti. The planned digital speedo and rev-counter were replaced by regular analogue instruments, and its avant-garde qualities were restricted to a pair of orange warning lights which glowed when the pre-set maximum revs or mph was reached. Another couple of hazard-warning lights featured on the steering column. Yellow signalled a minor inconvenience, red indicated there was a serious problem. The degree of urgency was translated by a panel to the left of the driver. This bore a schematic representation of the car, with glowing lights for all the key functions. If there was a problem, the corresponding light went out. Digital speedos and electronic dashboards were still things of the future, but Maserati made progress in this direction with the Quattroporte II instrumentation, although it was not a complete success. The line of show cars produced annually at Bertone continued to evolve the digital readout and computer-graph instrumentation, an example being the Alfa Romeo 33 Navajo prototype of 1976 which revealed its rev band in linear fashion.

The two-seater layout was state-of-the-art sports-racer, which in 1971 meant Porsche 917 and Ferrari 512, and harked back to the mid to late-'60s Ford GT40, Lola T70, Ferrari P3/4 and, indeed, the Muira itself. The driving

An unusual colour, maroon, but popular for certain Italian classic cars. This is Mike Pullen's ultra-low 1979 LP 400 S, which has a ride-height some one-and-a-half inches lower than standard. Mike used this car to great effect on the 1990 London to Venice Challenge, seeing off many other supercars, including the odd Ferrari F40, of course

Just arrived in the UK, this 25th Anniversary model seen from head on demonstrates how much the styling has evolved in a decade or so. Compare it with the LP 400 5 (pic 33), and see how the rear-view mirrors stand further out, the wiper parks left, the driving lamps are set lower in the air dam, there are now brake cooling ducts in the skirting, and the radiator cooling ducts are more prominent

Above

Some members will go to any lengths to protect their pride and joy, and think of all the natural oils which might be deposited

Left

Slatted radiator air intake ducts are restyled for the 25th Anniversary model. Originally introduced as a result of a quest for better cooling in 1973 when the LP 400 took over from the LP 500 prototype, which at that point had completely flush louvres at this point. The radiators which had originally been laid flat alongside the engine were now effectively stood on end and linked by a cross-over system

position was thus semi-recumbent. The seats were separated by a massive central transmission tunnel, the gearbox itself in fact, and this swas heavily padded like the surprisingly slim sill sections. The front wheel arches intruded boldly at calf-level.

Outside, the Countach looked like some brooding alien sling shot. Gandini majored on the geometric form of the trapezium to arrive at the basic shape, and placing the radiators at the rear of the car, racing fashion, made the ultra-low nose possible. If the outer image of the car wasn't enough to stop you in your tracks, the butterfly-wing doors would get you. Where as a gullwing door like the Mercedes 300SL's pivoted on the roofline, the Countach's doors were front-hinged but lifted vertically by an hydraulic arrangement. It was an

Above

This immaculate black 25th Anniversary Countach belongs to Ben Pollard, and the bird's eye view gives a clear idea of the refined aerodynamic shape of the rear wing. What is less clear perhaps, is how they came to paint Miuras such strange colours in the late '60s. Lime green, orange and lemon yellow were just three hues of a variety favoured by Lamborghini, in those far off days of psychedelic power

Right

A black bull from Bologna stands outside the marquee of British concessionaires Portman Lamborghini Limited at their Silverstone test day. Under the auspices of David Joliffe, the new Portman company took over from the old in October 1992. Lamborghinis have entered the country via Portman since 1984, and indeed many of the original personnel go way back to 1971 when Portman was the London dealer. The original UK concessionaire was Berlinetta Italia Ltd, of Whyteleafe, Surrey, with Maltin of Henley-on-Thames being the only other British outlet

expensive solution to manufacturing a door opening system, but practical in the sense that you can perhaps avoid door scrapes when alighting. But should you make the mistake of venturing into a multi-storey, you'll get stuck! Drivers had better think twice about keeping it in a regular garage. If you want a precedent for this remarkable ostentation, Gandini did it before with the Bertone-produced prototype Alfa Romeo Carabo, displayed at the Paris Salon in 1968. This dart-like 2.0-litre V8 was a mass of louvres for the rear screen, headlights and air intake, and entry was via the butterfly-wing doors, a direct ancestor for the Countach.

Whilst the concept of Carabo and Countach was broadly similar, Gandini avoided the louvres of the Alfa show car for the Lamborghini, apart from the engine cooling ducts, and gave the LP 500 Countach pop-up headlights, fared-in indicators and side-lights, and an intriguing double tunnel treatment for rear window and rear mirror vision. The mirror channel echoed the perspective of the window, in miniature, giving it an altogether neat effect.

The original cutaway shape of the rear wheel arches surfaced recently with Gandini's Maserati Shamal. The wheels they housed on LP 500 were shod with the same 60-section Pirellis as the Miura SV, although contemporary 'wet' racing tyres perhaps would have looked more appropriate. The tyre selection question is crucial in supercar design. Dallara, who was retained as a consultant went so far as to describe the Pirelli P7 in 1978 as "the greatest single breakthrough in motoring history". Pirelli even claimed that the Countach S was redesigned around the P7 tyre. The space-saver spare was carried in the nose; luggage room was minimal but there was a boot in the rear of the car, aft of the engine.

Stanzani, Parenti and Wallace evolved a development programme which took in intensive motoring on two test tracks, the Autodromo Modena and the Varano di Melegari. For road evaluation they used a hilly section of the old Mille Miglia route between Bologna and Florence, taking in the Raticosa and Futa passes. One of the longest trips was taken by Stanzani and Wallace to the Targa Florio in May 1972, to see the lone works Ferrari 312P driven to victory by Munari and Merzario. A neat irony is that ex-World Rally Champion Sandro Munari is currently Lamborghini's public relations supremo. It was a bold step to go testing so far from home, on a route encompassing every obstacle that the Italian and Sicilian road network could throw up. But LP 500 took it all in its stride, with no problems. Back on the Autodromo Modena, telemetry was

Dusky pink LP 500 S of 1982, bought new from Sant'Agata Bolognese by present owner Jeff White. The special colour scheme was arrived at simply by asking Marketing Director Ubaldo Sgarzi to copy the colour of his girlfriend's sweat-shirt for the body of the car and her blue belt for its upholstery. The Italian is reputed to have questioned the Englishman's sanity, in the nicest possible way, of course

checked and evaluated with an on-board recorder, and in the absence of a factory wind-tunnel, they simply stuck tufts of wool all over the upper surfaces of one side of the body and drove it at speed, with the effects recorded from a camera car travelling alongside. It wasn't so much that there were doubts about the aerodynamic efficiency of Gandini's design, but because of the original longitudinal set-up of the radiators, there were engine cooling problems and they needed to try different configurations for new cooling ducts supplying the revised transverse layout. The purity of Gandini's shape was compromised to an extent, but along with NACA cooling ducts in the flanks, the new air boxes simply served to render the car more outrageous.

Every manufacturer has to submit a prototype for crash testing in order to gain what is known as 'Type Approval', necessary in order to have permission to sell the model in quantity in any given country. The crash-test ensures that the chassis can withstand severe impacts, and the steering column movement can be measured. An important consideration in the case of the Countach was how the butterfly-wing doors would behave; if they jammed shut in an accident the occupants could be trapped inside, so the hinge arrangement incorporated linch-pins which could be removed with a ring-pull in the event of the normal opening mechanism failing. There are a host of type approval regulations to be met. For instance, any external projections are tested to see how they might affect a wayward pedestrian, but the Countach doesn't have many of these; tyres come under scrutiny; glass standards have to be observed; and engine decibels are monitored. The crash test is an expensive but unavoidable consideration for a small manufacturer so the LP 500 was shipped to MIRA, the Motor Industry Research Association's premises at Nuneaton, wired to an array of monitors then catapulted into a concrete wall. In the impact the front subframe was destroyed up to the axle line and the bodywork crumpled to the bulkhead.

Meanwhile, behind the scenes a production car was being prepared. It would be hand-made and incorporate all the data gathered from testing the LP 500. A space-frame chassis using tubes reminiscent of scaffold poles was built up by Modena chassis specialist Marchesi, and a slightly less complicated and thinner gauge frame which was clad in unstressed aluminium panels was added to this complex triangulated cage. The floorpan was made of glassfibre, and lightweight toughened Belgian Gleverbel glass was used to keep the weight down. Small three-quarter side windows slanted away into the air-intake channels. The high standards required of the Countach in handling and roadholding were taken

What may seem at first a broad expanse of a race circuit grows suddenly narrower once you let loose 450bhp of thundering red monster. Here Vic Sawyer storms along the track at Castle Combe intent on blowing some of the cobwebs out of his trusty 5000 Qv

53

Above
When this mid-'70s BMW 3.0 CSL in hot Countach pursuit was new, Lamborghini was just releasing the LP 400. So could a race-spec BMW hold a candle to the 5000 Qv? In the corners, very likely, but down the straights, forget it!

Left
A black 5000 Qv swings across and prepares to kiss the apex at Camp Bend, Castle Combe, before exiting past the paddock onto the start-finish straight

Overleaf
Surely this says what driving the Countach is all about – Vic Sawyer flat out on the Hangar Straight at Silverstone

Above

Is that tyre smoke or are things getting a bit overheated under the engine cover? A 5000 S driver on the limit at Woodcote tries everything he knows to haul in the competition 911 up ahead

Right

Hammering through the chicane complex and into Silverstone's Woodcote bend, a white 5000 Qv harries a later red Anniversary model. Shame there are no crowds to witness the spectacle

care of at the front end by double wishbones, coil springs and special fully-adjustable Koni dampers, and double anti-roll bars were mounted behind the front axle. At the rear there were single transverse upper links and lower wishbones, with twin coil spring-damper units on each side. The original magnesium hub-carriers were liable to break up, and cars were recalled soon after they went into production for new alloy replacements to be fitted. Braking was by exotic four-pot calliper Girling 18/4 discs, straight from the race track.

Many other revisions were incorporated. There would be two wipers on the first of the new cars, and there would be air intakes in the nose for cooling the front brakes; revised wheels were shod with Michelin XWX boots. The rear-view mirror no longer worked like a periscope, and the roof was flattened off. The rear lights were rationalised into framed units within the characteristic

panels, and the instrument panel came right back down to earth with a neatly boxed array of US-made Stewart Warner gauges. The major re-think was in the motive power department. It was all very well having the increased power of the 5.0-litre engine, but far more sensible would be to use the existing 4.0-litre unit with all the advantages of ready-made component supply and long-term reliability. The drive-train was still by the same inter-sump arrangement developed for the 5.0-litre engine, with transmission taken through a Fichtel and Sachs Porsche 917-type clutch to a five-speed indirect gearbox. Magnesium was used regularly for items like the sump, clutch housings and gearbox casings in an effort to maintain low unsprung weight.

The Countach now became the LP 400, in deference to the engine swap. The 4.0-litre lump quenched its thirst through two sets of three twin-choke sidedraught Weber 45 DCOE 23 carburettors. There were now two Marelli distributors instead of the single one for the LP 500. The new cooling system was backed up by a thermostat-controlled fan plus another controlled by the driver, and an oil cooler was mounted in the right front wing. Each engine was meticulously put together by a single man, a practice intended to avoid errors and build pride in the workforce. Machining was done at the point of assembly, and the car in-build proceeded round the 'U'-shaped factory on a system of rails, pushed along by hand.

The pre-production cherry-red LP 400 was dispatched to the 1973 Geneva Show, and the second LP 400, finished in green, had bigger air intakes and as a result, a slightly bigger nose, which also housed driving lamps. This car also had what was to become the characteristic single parallelogram windscreen wiper. This model was shown at the Paris salon later in the year. Three years on from the debut of the LP 500, the first production LP 400 rolled out of Sant'Agata to be launched at the 1974 Geneva show. It was sold to industrialist Walter Wolf, its white paintwork in stark contrast to Wolf's midnight blue Grand Prix cars. The first year's production was spoken for, and Stanzani was led to believe by the management that they could sell 50 cars a year.

What constitutes a supercar? Well, bags of muscle from an exotic, multi-cylinder engine; eye-catching broad-shouldered looks; two snug seats; an uncompromising ride; and scant regard for creature comforts

Above

This white Qv is in marked contrast to the very first Lamborghini car which was based on a Fiat Topolino, with its engine size increased from 500cc to 750cc. In 1948, with Baglioni as co-drlver, Feruccio Lamborghini entered the awesome Mille Miglia race. The car was retired, but a number of interested parties asked for copies. However, his personal fortune was to be made building tractors

Left

Steve Forster pits his 25th Anniversary model against the demanding new complex section at Silverstone. Out on the circuit, these club outings are serious occasions, even for roadgoing cars, and demand medical attendance and marshalling. Drivers must wear up-to-date crash helmets too

Above

On a club day at Castle Combe, the chequered flag indicates the end of a session rather than a race. This is Steve Ashton's LP 400 S, a 1982 car originally owned by Tim Dutton who made the eponymous kit cars. When Steve Ashton bought the car it was equipped with a wing, but this was abandoned during a respray from the original gold to the present subtle blue colour

Left

The Countach was designated the LP 500 in prototype form, which stood for Longitudinal Posteriore 5.0-litre. Engineer Stanzani and his team made several important changes during the Countach's development. The 5.0-litre engine originally used was down-sized to the previous 4.0-litre V12 as there were doubts about its reliability. It expanded once again to 5.0-litres, later gaining 4-valves per cylinder, and was finally upped to 5.2-litres for the 5000 quattrovalvole and Anniversary model

Above
Quite at home on the circuit, the Countach's supple chassis is a hefty multi-tubular spaceframe layout. In the first place, the main reason for placing the engine longitudinally rather than transversely was to counteract the Miura's twitchiness at high speed and in cross winds

Right
Two 25th Anniversary models plus a Diablo simmer in the pits at Silverstone during the Portman Concessionaires track day in October 1991. All manner of exotic machinery was present during this event including racing motorcycles and a racing Porsche 911

Above
Long-time Lamborghini owner and enthusiast, Peter Hay is Chairman of the Lamborghini Club UK. Here he enjoys the camaraderie of club day in the paddock at Silverstone

Left
Outside, the Countach 5000 Qv looked like a brooding alien sling shot. Gandini used the geometric form of the trapezium to arrive at the basic shape, by placing the radiators at the rear of the car, sports-racing fashion, he made the ultra-low nose possible

PRODUCTION TAKES OFF

During the first three years of production, 150 LP 400 Countachs left the factory. Like most small-scale operations, supply could not meet demand. Wallace was long gone, and Stanzani gave up trying to co-ordinate an increasingly difficult schedule of work and to satisfy a less than competent management. It was at this point that Dallara reappeared to develop the 'S' model. He began, perversely, with the new low-profile Pirelli P7 tyre rearranging the suspension and improving the brakes to match its tenacious properties. Now the Campagnolo 'telephone-dial' wheelrims, 81/2J at the front and 12 inches wide at the rear, carried 205/50 VR 15 and 345/35 VR-15 P7s respectively, and the wheel arches had to wear matching moulded fibreglass spats to cover the wider rubber. The character of the car was changed at a stroke from lithe road-runner to macho street-racer. The spats round the front arches were extended effectively to introduce a full-width chin spoiler, manufactured in-unit with the front panel. Out went the stylish periscope rear-view mirror arrangement and the lid was smoothed over. Ordinary door mirrors had to suffice, for there could be no looking back through the massive 12-cylinder engine.

Aesthetic considerations aside, it was the suspension changes which counted. At the front, springs and dampers were relocated to decrease the camber and roll angles, and a thicker anti-roll bar was added. Pairs of twin parallel lower links replaced the wishbones at the back, in order to counteract adverse rear axle movement caused by tyre flex during cornering. ATE brake callipers took the place of the Girling jobs acting on the massive ventilated discs, and there were changes to bearings, hub carriers, and steering box. Inside, the controls were improved to include a hinged accelerator pedal and the positioning of the handbrake lever was switched from left to right of the driver. Not surprisingly, the Countach felt like a big piece of machinery to put through its paces, and was an intimidating prospect for the uninitiated. Steering was heavy and gear changes were apt to be awkward. But handling was sharp, veering to understeer, the chassis felt supple and there was little body roll. The fat P7s afforded plentiful grip. For those wishing to get seriously acquainted

Two generations of Lamborghini: Peter Hay's silver 25th Anniversary model, bought direct from the factory in March 1990 and his yellow Miura, a car he also bought new 18 years before in 1972. Styled by Gandini whilst still a Bertone employee, the Miura was to revolutionise sports car design, being the first of the modern generation of supercars. The P400 Miura was special as it brought mid-engined sports-racing car layout to the street. The 4.0-litre V12 was mounted in the transverse position behind the passenger compartment, and its top speed was 160 mph

with the fast lane, there was no longer any trace of wandering at high speed, a vice which had afflicted the Miura and early Countachs.

Despite the fact that the management was in turmoil for most of the decade, the Countach continued to evolve, and in late 1979 the Series 2 S came out. With control passing over to the Mimram family, consultant engineer Giulio Alfieri became Chief Engineer and manager of the Sant'Agata plant. Lamborghini was entering a period of stability. Not that the Countach's appearance suggested this, because the latest fashionable accoutrement was the outrageous rear wing, quickly embellished with endplates. The wing or aerofoil was mounted on the rear of the luggage boot lid. It was an option at first, but soon buyers had to specify if they didn't want one. Was it a piece of cosmetic gimmickry, or did it stabilise the car at speed? The suspension was jacked up slightly to improve ground-clearance, but a wing was hardly needed to cope with this. The S 2 also featured a zany steering wheel with oval holes, and a bigger dashboard with larger instruments including a speedo in mph and kmh.

The LP 400 S was nearing the end of the line, however, because weight gains and emission controls had conspired to sap the power output from 375bhp to nearer 340bhp. Alfieri's solution was to increase bore and stroke and get close to the 5.0-litres again. Capacity rose from 3929cc to 4754cc, and output was back up to 375bhp again. The revised engine used electronic ignition, and the gearbox was treated to a set of taller ratios. The LP 500 was ready for the 1982 Geneva Show, although externally nothing had changed apart from the identification on the rear of the car.

During the '80s, the Countach was indisputably the standard-bearer, but Lamborghini was still active in other areas. In 1982 another junior supercar was launched, the neat and compact Jalpa, whose wheel arches mimicked the Countach. Power came from a 3.5-litre V8, and a replacement for this model was well underway in 1992. Going into territory explored earlier by a four-wheel-drive vehicle designed for the military and called the Cheetah, Lamborghini introduced the LMA 002, a monstrous off-roader with dramatic angular styling, powered by a 7.0-litre V12. It was aimed largely at the wealthy Arab market. Other areas of business have included powerboat engines, a record company and Swiss watches.

Rivals in the supercar league were few and far between. Some, like the Porsche 911 Turbo, ran out of steam long before the Countach's theoretical192mph maximum, although by the end of the decade, the 959, a four-wheel-drive technological masterpiece, was capable of 197mph. Stylistically, only Ferrari was in the hunt, first with the flat-12-engined 4.4-litre

The 5000 Qv is Vic Sawyer's fourth Countach. Vic, a large-scale professional roofing contractor, entered the exalted world of the supercar owner with a 308GT/4 in 1978. He hosted the club gathering where this picture was taken

365 GT/4 BB, made from 1973 to 1976. From 1976 the LP 400's principal competition took the form of the Ferrari 512 Berlinetta Boxer, although the DeTomaso Pantera, in GT5S form running with a 5.7-litre stock Ford V8, achieved supercar looks and performance without the same degree of sophistication. And it was nearly half the price. In 1984 Ferrari had the Testarossa, now running with a re-engineered version of the four-cam 5.0-litre boxer engine. There were four-valves per cylinder, and power output was 390bhp at 6300rpm.

A year later at the Geneva Show, Lamborghini had matched the Testarossa with a brand-new 48-valve version of the V12 engine installed in the LP 500. All the internals, like pistons, rods and crank were new, and the stroke was lengthened slightly to bring the engine up to 5167cc. The bhp soared to a silky-smooth 455 at 7000rpm, making the Countach, for a while at least, the fastest road-car in the world. You could buy a piece of the action for £67,000, or if you couldn't quite run to that, the Qv's little sister, the equally talented Jalpa was available for £32,500. Downdraught 44DCNF Webers were employed on the Qv engine, and the breathing was immediately improved. Noisy it may have been, but it was the sort of noise to gladden the heart of any supercar

Above
There's no question which is the fastest means of transport; it's the one which doesn't get involved with traffic jams or the long arm of the law. The Countach on the other hand provides rather more in the way of thrills at ground level

Right
By the time they reached the 5000 S, the rear-view mirror had long since ceased to work like a periscope, and the roof was flattened off. The rear lights were rationalised into framed units within those characteristic panels, and rear wings sprouted

Above

The Countach ceased production in 1990 with the Anniversary model, and has been superseded by the Diablo. Gandini took many of the styling elements of the Countach and worked them into his new design, to produce a supercar for the '90s, just as outrageous as the Countach was in 1973

Left

The Countach's prodigious size has always made it a difficult vehicle to negotiate winding, narrow country lanes. Dimensions are difficult to judge from the cocoon of the cockpit, and are all a matter of experience. For the record, it is 13ft 6ins long, 6ft 6ins wide, and just 3ft 6ins high

enthusiast. A ZF syncromesh gearbox took the place of the Porsche-sourced transmission, and Oz wheels took over from Campagnolo.

Ferrari stole the honours once again, this time with the F40. Its twin-turbo V8 pumped out 478bhp, just topping 200mph, and its Group C racing car looks surpassed the LP 500. This was, arguably, the first time anything had beaten the Countach on both looks and performance, although to be fair, the spartan F40 was not as pleasant to ride in as the LP 500 because of noise levels and an uncompromising ride. The Countach's styling had aged well however, and to celebrate the company's quarter century as a motor manufacturer, Lamborghini took the capacity up to 5.2-litres and introduced the Countach 25 Anniversary model, which with the Diablo waiting in the wings, was to be the car's swansong.

The already extravagant body was now kitted out with skirts, or sill extensions, and colour-coded bumpers, which may well have been deemed unnecessary appendages, but were not out of place bearing in mind the late '80s obsession with body kits. The interior was updated, with electronically controlled seats and an improved ventilation system going some way to off-setting what had always been a deficit, the lack of headroom in the claustrophobic cabin. If by now you're hooked on the Countach, be certain to have a good relationship with your bank manager. New, a Countach 25 would set you back £98,957, but as they made only 400 of this run-out model, there would be a substantial premium on that figure.

Lamborghini had been under the protective wing of the US Chrysler Corporation since September 1987, allowing the company to go its own way. Thus there was still an atmosphere of autonomy about the firm. The Countach ceased production in 1989, and was superseded by the Diablo. It would be

In 17 years, the Countach's styling had aged well, and to celebrate the company's quarter century as a motor manufacturer, Lamborghini introduced the Countach 25th Anniversary, which, with the Diablo waiting in the wings, was to be the car's swansong. Its already extravagant body was kitted out with skirts and colour-coded bumpers. Mike Lake's LP 400 ahead of Vic Sawyer's Qv represent two earlier generations of Countach

78

They believe in starting them young at Lamborghini. He's probably hooked for good. Once an enthusiast, always an enthusiast

over-simplifying things to say that Gandini took all the styling elements of the Countach and worked them into a new design, because Chrysler's design team gave the concept a final going over. But essentially that's what you got; a supercar for the '90s, as outrageous as the Countach was in 1973, but with all the airscoops and add-ons superbly integrated and smoothed over.

Above left

An impromptu gathering of Countachs attracts an inevitable crowd. This time they're outside the celebrated Hard Rock Cafe near Hyde Park Corner in London's Mayfair. A 5000 Qv heads the orderly parade

Left

Stately Georgian and Regency facades provide a sober backdrop for the muscle-bound bunch of supercars, comprising three Quattrovalvole and a pair of Anniversaries

Above

By now joined by a sixth party-goer this dramatic nocturnal shot works wonders for the English Tourist Board. It must have been a good meal at the Hard Rock because late in the evening, the team's still there; convenient parking, but it helps if you know the manager

Above

The split-rim wheel was a result of racing technology. It is light and versatile, and better still, being of two separate sections, the rim could be swapped if damaged, or if a different width was required. In this case, it complements the dramatic Countach styling admirably

Right

Happy Anniversary. Considering the amount of magnesium used in the Countach's manufacture, silver is an appropriate colour. Items like the sump, clutch housings and gearbox casings and original hub carriers were all cast in magnesium in an effort to maintain low unsprung weight

Above

The gearbox was placed ahead of the engine with a return shaft directed back through a sealed lubrication channel in the deeper, more heavily ribbed sump to the differential. The gearbox was now right by the driver's gear-changing hand, so the need for linkage control rods was removed

Left

The interior and controls of the Anniversary model were a far cry from the futuristic concept of the prototype LP 500, which was originally planned to have a digital speedo and rev-counter. The only avant-garde element was limited to a pair of orange warning lights which glowed when the pre-set maximum revs or mph was reached. A panel beside the driver carried a plan of the car, which had warning lights glowing for all the key functions

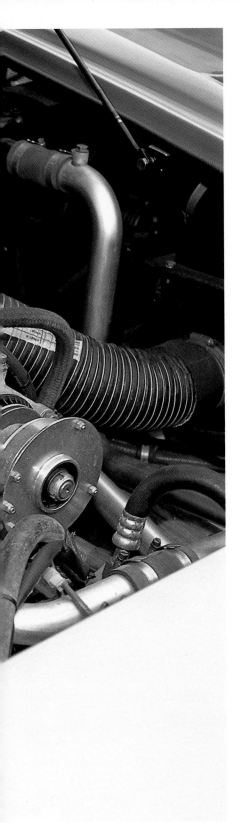

Above

It wasn't always this good for Lamborghini. In the early '70s the looks, the performance and the handling may have been right, but the firm was beset with industrial disputes and strikes. What's more, Lamborghinis were getting a reputation for inadequate finishing, particularly in their interiors. Some British buyers took their cars straight to one of the leading coach builders to have the interior removed and replaced with something rather more carefully made

Left

Prototype LP 500 used a 5.0-litre engine, but it was decided to use the existing tried and tested 4.0-litre unit which had the advantage of ready-made component supply. The drive-train was still by the same inter-sump arrangement developed for the 5.0-litre engine, with transmission taken through a Fichtel and Sachs clutch to a five-speed gearbox, and in 1973 the Countach became the LP 400. The Anniversary engine seen here has been boosted again to 5.2-litres and equipped with four-valve heads

Left

Lamborghini chose his own zodiac sign for his company logo: Taurus the Bull, and in a typically rampant, bullish sort of way, he tackled Ferrari's prancing horse head on. In retirement he went on to produce his own label of wine – Bull's Blood

Below

Marcello Gandini's career began in 1959 when he produced the body for an OSCA Barchetta, but his big break came when Giugiaro left Bertone and he was asked to fill the vacated position of chief designer. Apart from the Countach, he went on to style the classic Muira and, subsequently, the Lamborghini Marzal, Espada and Jalpa, the Ferrari 308GT4, Maserati Khamsin, Lancia Stratos, Innocenti Mini, Fiat X-I/9, and Citroen BX. More recently he has drawn the Maserati Shamal, Cizeta Moroder and Lamborghini Diablo

The LP 400 was said to have been designed around a revolutionary new tyre, the Pirelli P7. Squat and of low profile, this tyre took motoring into a new dimension of handling and grip. This OZ wheel shows evidence of occasional kerbing; hard to park, these Countachs

Above
New, a Countach 25 would set you back a reasonable £98,957

Left
Steve Forster's 25th Anniversary looks so good, it's easy to forget the 1970s were difficult years for the motor industry with many firms closing down. At Lamborghini, this period reached rock bottom when the owner had the company declared bankrupt. Enter the Mimram family, who leased the Sant'Agata plant to keep the business going before buying it when the receivers put the company up for auction in 1980

Above
Underneath every Countach lurks a tubular space-frame chassis, built up by Modena chassis specialist Marchesi. Another less complicated and thinner gauge frame is added to the basic chassis, and clad in unstressed aluminium panels. The floorpan is made of glassfibre, and lightweight toughened glass is used to keep the weight down

Left
Gandini's most radical design, the Countach still looked as stunning in 1990 as it did in 1971. The extravagant nature of that original concept should have militated against a long aesthetic shelf life: the car should look really look embarassing by now...

Above

With the advent of the 5000, certain changes were made to the suspension. Up front, springs and dampers were relocated to decrease camber and roll angles, and a thicker anti-roll bar was added. Twin parallel lower links replaced the wishbones at the back, to counteract rear axle movement when the tyres flexed during cornering. All ball-joints were fully-adjustable

Right

The dihedral rear wing and those 'telephone-dial' wheelrims are a Countach trademark, 81/2J at the front and 12 inches wide at the rear, more than likely wearing 205/50 VR 15 and 345/35 VR-15 Pirelli P7s respectively, and the wheel arches are clad in matching moulded fibreglass spats to cover the wide boots

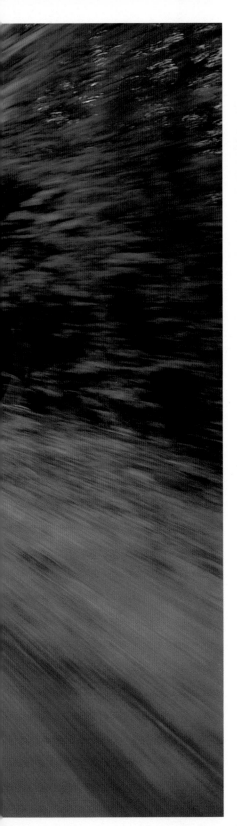

Above
Hauling down nearly a ton-and-a-half from well over twice the legal limit calls for very special braking properties. Four-pot ATE brake callipers do the business on the massive ventilated discs

Left
So how does it feel to be out there in charge of a 5000 Qv? Steering feels heavy at low speed, but is very direct and kart-like at high velocity, with plenty of feed-back. The gear change can feel stiff, and on earlier cars the pedals required some effort. But although it can be a demanding mistress, handling is sharp, veering to understeer, and the chassis is supple with little body roll. Trust in those fat Pirellis to provide plenty of trip, but wise to lay off the throttle in the wet

Above

This modern-day black beauty is Rick Lee's 1988-spec 5000 Qv, the penultimate model in the Countach evolution. There was a fad for painting performance cars in black around this time, but it has always been a good colour and only adds to the aggressive mystery of the beast

Right

The shapely door mirror goes wherever the door points. The stylish periscope arrangement, a feature of the early cars was just not good enough and disappeared with the last of the LP 400 S models in 1982

Fabulous interior upholstered in leather cossets driver and passenger, and the light colour lends a feeling of roominess, avoiding any tendency to feel claustrophobic. Few windscreens slope as sharply as this, and the tall driver is the victim of restricted headroom

Above

It is hard to credit that these are stable mates; a little like David and Goliath, the 5000 Qv is dwarfed by the angular bulk of the LM002, Lamborghini's vast off-roader. This 7.0-litre giant was developed from an original four-wheel-drive project called the Cheetah, intended for military application. The LM002 found buyers primarily among the wealthy and extravagant in the Middle East

Left

Minimal ground clearance here, and the low-slung look is emphasised by the side skirts and air dam. Cooling ducts abound, for there are channels in the body-kit for fresh air to reach both front and rear brakes

Overleaf

Rick Lee's 5000 Qv is descended from the LP 400 S, which eventually succumbed to weight gains and power-sapping emission controls, dropping the power output from 375bhp to 340bhp. By increasing bore and stroke, capacity was lifted to 5.0-litres once more, and output was back up to 375bhp. In came electronic ignition and a taller set of gear ratios, and the LP 500 was ready for the 1982 Geneva Show

Above

Fans are unable to contain themselves as Mike Pullen's LP 400 S comes among them at sunny Goodwood. Despite that ground-hugging nose, a full-size spare wheel could be carried, mainly because there was no frontal radiator to accommodate, unlike Ferrari BB and Porsche 911 competition

Right

Lambos in line: a pair of LP 400 S Countachs flank a 5000 Qv on the track at Goodwood. The older cars belong to Mike Pullen and Steve Ashton and the smart red example in the middle is piloted by Roger Hawkins

Above

The sports-racing wedge was an obvious shape for performance cars when the Countach LP 500 first appeared, and it was also employed by BMW, Maserati, Lancia, Lotus and TVR. Despite its overtly streamlined appearance, the Countach drag coefficient is a high Cd of 0.41. The Diablo betters this considerably at Cd 0.31, and the lack of wind tunnel facilities two decades ago has much to do with this inequitable state of affairs

Left

Lights ablaze on the track at Goodwood at the command of the author. But inevitably, pop-up headlights are ungainly and do nothing for the Countach's lines. They're best kept out of sight until darkness beckons

Above
Small, extrovert motor manufacturers like Lamborghini and Lotus are always prime candidates for take over, Chrysler finalised just such a deal with Lamborghini in September 1987. This extra muscle allowed a new plant to be installed at Sant'Agata Bolognese (so that the Diablo could be developed) reputedly for the relatively modest sum of £10 million

Left
Feruccio Lamborghini himself was always reluctant to go racing with his own cars, which is why Dallara left to design the DeTomaso Grand Prix car. However, Lamborghini has supplied engines to the Lotus, Lola, Minardi, and Larrousse Venturi Formula 1 teams, with what is best described as fair success. Development costs estimated at £5 million are modest by current FI standards, but since racing improves the breed, future Lamborghinis can only benefit

Overleaf
Unlike the Countach which was always painstakingly built and finished by hand, its successor the Diablo has the advantage of having its main underframe constructed on a jig. Chassis tubes are in square sections rather than round, and whereas certain Countach panels like the door skins were in aluminium, the Diablo uses stronger light alloy. They are also stamped instead of being hand-beaten

Left

Dynamics of a Countach on full song: solid acceleration; whirring valvegear drowned by a deepening growl; bags of torque tempered by traction from ample rubber; and you're suddenly hurtling down the road at breakneck speed

Overleaf

The search for a successor to the Countach began in 1985. The brief was similar to that for the Miura and Countach – to get as far out as possible on the outer limits of stylistic reason. Gandini's design became a full-size model by June 1986, but approval for the Diablo's final format was in Chrysler's hands

Above

No denying the Anniversary has put on weight, looking visibly bulkier than her predecessors. The body-kit brought the styling in line with contemporaries in the car parks of late '80s fashionable watering holes

Right

Rear three-quarter vision is virtually non-existent; the tiny side-rear window affords a good view of the air intake, so if you're unsure of what lies behind and you need to reverse, Portman Concessionaires' Peter Leonard Morgan provides a 'how to' demonstration. It may look unorthodox, but it saves on the insurance claims

Giving the fabulous Anniversary model an airing, with every aperture open to the elements

Above
The Orangery at Syon Park is the setting for the first and last of the Countachs to be imported into the UK; one is an LP 400, the other an Anniversary. The lines of the earlier car are cleaner and uncluttered, and in some ways are less aggressive

Left
In 1977 the LP 400 would have set you back £30,000; the last of the 25th Anniversary costing over three times that amount at nearly £99,000

Above
That distinctive cutaway rear wheel arch is so much more prominent in the LP 400, unencumbered by the fibreglass spats added later. It is a Gandini trademark, turning up again more recently in the Maserati Shamal

Above left
Engineer's dream or rich man's plaything; how many Countachs were exploited to their full potential, reaching 100mph in less than 12 seconds or 180mph-plus top speed? It needed 4000rpm on the rev counter before it really took off, but has been a favourite with the local constabulary

Left
All Countach engines are run-in on the Sant'Agata dynamometer prior to installation, ensuring that each of these marvels of Italian engineering operates as advertised

Technical Specifications

Countach S, 1977

MANUFACTURER

Automobili Ferruccio Lamborghini Spa
40019 Sant'Agata Bolognese
Bologna, Italy

GENERAL

Curb weight, lb 3020
Test weight 3230
Weight distribution (with driver),
 front/rear, % 43/57
Wheelbase, in. 96.5
Track, front/rear 59.1/59.8
Length 163.0
Width 74.4
Height 42.1
Ground clearance 4.9
Overhang, front/rear 36.7/29.8
Usable trunk space, cu ft 7.5
Fuel capacity, U.S. gal. 31.7

ENGINE

Type dohc V-12
Bore x stroke, mm 82.0 x 62.0
Equivalent in. 3.23 x 2.44
Displacement, cc/cu in. 3929/240
Compression ratio 10.5:1
Bhp @ rpm, DIN 375 @ 8000
Equivalent mph 192
Torque @ rpm, DIN, lb-ft 266 @ 5000
Carburetion six Weber 45 DCOE (2V)
Fuel requirement premium, 98-oct

DRIVETRAIN

Transmission 5-sp manual
Gear ratios: 5th (0.78) 3.19:1
4th (0.99) 4.05:1
3rd (1.31) 5.36:1
2nd (1.77) 7.24:1
1st (2.26) 9.24:1
Final drive ratio 4.09:1

ACCOMMODATION

Seating capacity, persons 2
Seat width 2 x 14.0
Head room 34.5
Seat back adjustment, deg 0

CHASSIS & BODY

Layout mid-engine/rear drive
Body/frame tubular steel
chassis/aluminium panels
Brake system 10.5-in. vented discs front
 and rear, vacuum assisted
Swept area, sq in. 416
Wheels Campagnolo cast alloy;
 14 x 71/2JJ front, 14 x 9JJ rear
Tyres Michelin XWX; 205/70VR-14 f,
 215/70-14 r
Steering type rack & pinion
Turns, lock-to-lock 3.0
Turning circle, ft 42.7
Front suspension: unequal length A-arms,
 coil springs, tube shocks, anti-roll bar
Rear suspension: upper lateral links,
 lower reversed A-arms, upper & lower
 trailing arms, dual coil springs, dual
 shock absorbers, anti-roll bar

INSTRUMENTATION

Instruments: 320-km/h speedo,
 9000-rpm tach, 99,999.9 odo,
 oil press, oil temp, coolant temp,
 ammeter, voltmeter, fuel level

Warning lights: brake sys, hand brake,
 alternator, a/c fan, a/c compressor,
 hazard, parking lights, high beam,
 directionals

CALCULATED DATA

Lb/bhp (test weight) 8.6
Mph/1000 rpm (5th gear) 23.3
Engine revs/mi (60 mph) 2570
Piston travel, ft/mi 1045
R&T steering index 1.28
Brake swept area, sq in./ton 258

ACCELERATION

Time to distance, sec:
 0-100 ft 3.2
 0-500 ft 8.1
 0-1320 ft (one-quarter mi) 14.6
Speed at end of one-quarter
 mi, mph 100.5
Time to speed, sec:
 0-30 mph 2.6
 0-50 mph 4.6
 0-60 mph 5.9
 0-70 mph 7.7
 0-100 mph 14.4
 0-110 mph 17.7

SPEEDS IN GEARS

5th gear (7500 rpm) est 164
4th (8000) 140
3rd (8000) 108
2nd (8000) 81
1st (8000) 64

FUEL ECONOMY
Normal driving, mpg 11.0
Cruising range, mi (1-gal. res) 338

HANDLING
Speed on 100-ft radius, mph 35.7
Lateral acceleration, g 0.852
Speed thru 700-ft slalom, mph 63.6

BRAKES
Minimum stopping distances, ft:
From 60 mph 131
From 80 mph 226
Control in panic stop excellent
Pedal effort for 0.5g stop, lb 15
*Fade: percent increase in pedal effort to
   maintain 0.5g deceleration in 6 stops
   from 60 mph nil*
Parking: hold 30% grade? no
Overall brake rating excellent

INTERIOR NOISE
All noise readings in dBA:
Idle in neutral 74
Maximum, 1st gear 102
Constant 30 mph 82
50 mph 85
70 mph 85
90 mph 88

*Information reproduced with kind
permission of Road & Track, December
1978. The road test talked of 'an eerie
stability that belies speeds of 100 plus'.*

*The last three right-hand drive Countachs to be imported into the UK arrive at
Portman Concessionaires depot*

No other car stirs the emotions like the Countach; visually it demands a response, and if you're aware of what powers it, you appreciate that its potential is awesome. And to drive it is to experience shattering performance, and not least, the rapt attentions of everyone who sees it